Ann Gregory
1938-1998

Tear cardstock in spiral circles to make flowers with dimension and form.

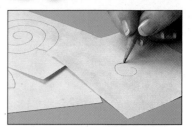

1. Trace or copy the pattern.

2. Make a line of water around the pattern.

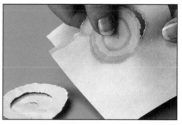

3. Tear the paper or cardstock.

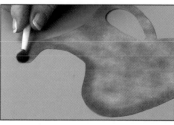

4. Chalk the edges if desired.

TEAR TOWARD
you to make a White edge.

TEAR AWAY
from you to keep a solid edge.

LEAF
PATTERN

by Laura Gregory

Our Friend - MATERIALS:
Keeping Memories Alive paper (Yellow square, Yellow check, Yellow stripe, Purple swirl, Green, Lavender) • *Creative Imaginations* butterfly paper • *Dayco* die-cut letters • Die-cut leaves • Computer generated lettering • Pop dots • Purple and Green chalk
TIPS: Layer torn flowers and attach with pop dots.

SPIRAL
FLOWER TOP
PATTERN

FLOWER BASE
PATTERN

Serendipity squares add elegance and color to your scrapbook page. Use cut squares for photo corners or punch shapes from serendipity paper... serendipity is special!

TAG
PATTERN
© Accu-Cut®

by Laura Gregory
Serendipity squares
created by Katrina Hogan
Japanese Gardens
MATERIALS: *Bazzill* cardstock (Black, White, Green, Dark Green, Sage Green) • *Colorbök* self-adhesive vellum (White, Cream print) • Die-cuts (*Far & Away* bamboo, *Accu-cut* tag) • *Stampin Up* leaf rubber stamp • Gold ink pad • Split ring • Dragonfly charm • Computer generated lettering

Our visit to
The Japanese
Water Gardens
April 2002

The Gregory
Family

by Christy Lemond
Serendipity squares
created by
Katrina Hogan

Philadelphia
MATERIALS: *Bazzill* paper (Navy Blue, Red, White and Tan cardstock, Blue mulberry) • *Worldwin* Red self adhesive vellum • *Stampin Up* 'Let Freedom Ring' rubber stamp • Black ink pad • *Accu-Cut* bell die-cut • Gray chalk • Black pen

our
Philadelphia
Trip

Fold

BELL
PATTERN
© Accu-Cut®

Cut along dashed line
on left side of bell.

Serendipity
Squares

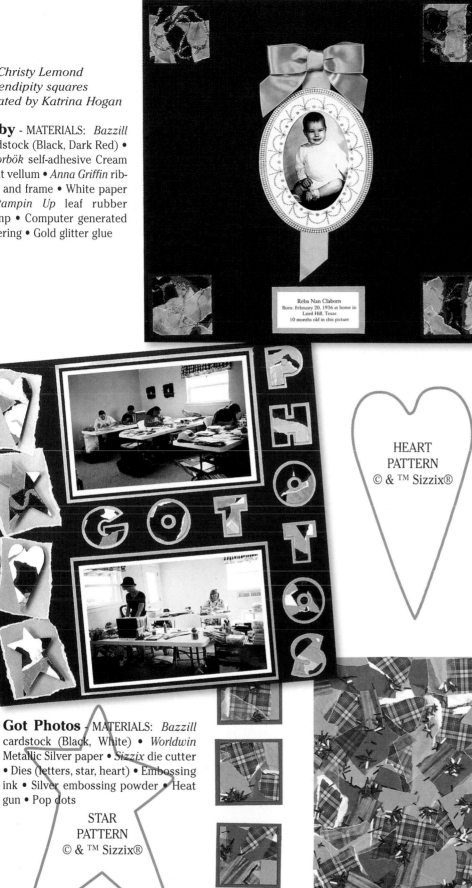

by Christy Lemond
Serendipity squares
created by Katrina Hogan

Baby - MATERIALS: *Bazzill* cardstock (Black, Dark Red) • *Colorbök* self-adhesive Cream print vellum • *Anna Griffin* ribbon and frame • White paper • *Stampin Up* leaf rubber stamp • Computer generated lettering • Gold glitter glue

Reba Nan Claborn
Born: February 20, 1936 at home in
Laird Hill, Texas
10 months old in this picture

HEART
PATTERN
© & ™ Sizzix®

Got Photos - MATERIALS: *Bazzill* cardstock (Black, White) • *Worldwin* Metallic Silver paper • *Sizzix* die cutter • Dies (letters, star, heart) • Embossing ink • Silver embossing powder • Heat gun • Pop dots

STAR
PATTERN
© & ™ Sizzix®

Serendipity Paper - MATERIALS: Cardstock (Gold, Dark Green) • Self-adhesive Brown plaid paper • Self-adhesive velum (leaf print, Orange) • Green Twistel • *Z Barten* Copper Jimmies • Glue

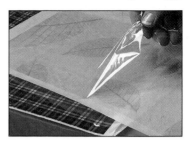

1. Choose papers and self-adhesive vellum.

2. Tear off pieces of paper and vellum, apply to background.

3. Continue adding paper pieces and Twistel.

4. Glue Jimmies on background in a random pattern.

5. Cut square of serendipity paper and mount on cardstock.

Shapes

by Laura Gregory

Turtle
MATERIALS: Green cardstock • Paper (*Keeping Memories Alive* Green fleck, Green check, White) • Black pen

by Laura Gregory

Gecko - MATERIALS: Paper (*Paper Adventures* Green print, Ivory) • 3 square Silver nailheads • 2 Green 8mm wiggle eyes

by Ruth Ann Warwick

Chick & Egg - MATERIALS: Cardstock (White, Yellow) • Black and Orange pens

by Laura Gregory

Frog - MATERIALS: Cardstock (Green, Hot Pink) • Gold crown nailhead • Two 12mm x 16mm wiggles eyes • ¼" spiral punch • Black pen

This collection of shapes is sure to contain just the right accent for a delightful, themed page. Just trace, transfer and tear!.

by Ruth Ann Warwick
Apple - MATERIALS: Cardstock (Red, Green, Brown)

by Ruth Ann Warwick
Straw Hat - MATERIALS: Cardstock (Dark Sage Green, Yellow) • Woven straw print paper • 26 gauge Green wire • Black pen

by Ruth Ann Warwick
Dog - MATERIALS: Cardstock (Brown, Red, Yellow) • Two 10mm wiggle eyes • Silver jump ring • 5/8" bone punch • Rust chalk • Black and Red pens

by Ruth Ann Warwick
Cross - MATERIALS: Cardstock (Sky Blue, Silver)

HOUSE PATTERNS

by Christy Lemond

Our Home - MATERIALS: *Bazzill* cardstock (Dark Brown, Light Blue, Green, Gray, Charcoal, White, Rust) • *Provo Craft* ⅞" wood letter stickers • Chalk (Blue, Black, Gray, Green)

STEP PATTERN

SHRUB PATTERNS

CLOUD PATTERNS

Love, marriage and home !

Our Wedding

CUTTING THE CAKE

JUST MARRIED

July 14, 2001

A cake, a house… make them to match your wedding colors or your home.

CAKE PATTERN

Show off your home with torn paper shapes. It's so easy!

by Christy Lemond

Our Wedding - MATERIALS: *Bazzill* White cardstock • *Daisy D's* Light Green/polka dot paper • *me & my BIG ideas* wedding stickers • *Jolee's* Pink flower stickers • 4mm White pearls by the yard • Pop dots • Pink chalk • Black pen

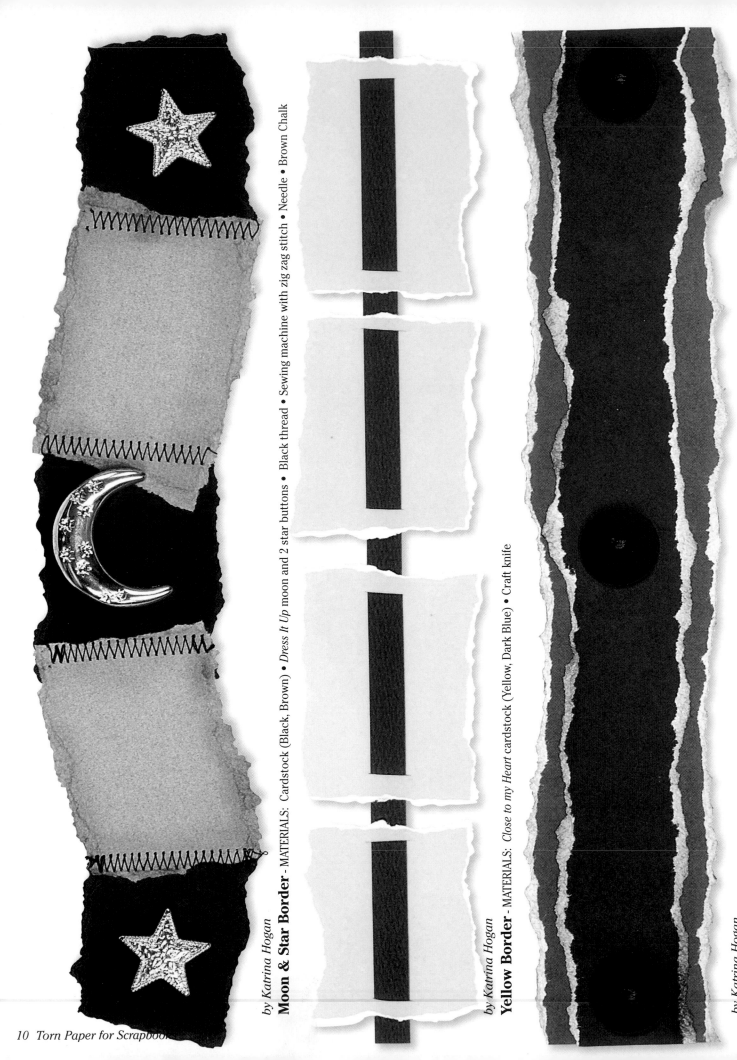

by Katrina Hogan
Moon & Star Border - MATERIALS: Cardstock (Black, Brown) • *Dress It Up* moon and 2 star buttons • Black thread • Sewing machine with zig zag stitch • Needle • Brown Chalk

by Katrina Hogan
Yellow Border - MATERIALS: *Close to my Heart* cardstock (Yellow, Dark Blue) • Craft knife

by Katrina Hogan
Button Border - MATERIALS: *Close to my Heart* cardstock (Pink, Green) • 3 *Making Memories* ⅞" Dark Green buttons • Green embroider floss • Needle • Pink and Green chalk

SISTERS

by Laura Gregory

Sisters - MATERIALS: *The Robin's Nest* paper (Yellow strip, Yellow print, Yellow, White, Black) • *Worldwin* vellum • *Stop N Crop* White fibers • White tassel • Die-cuts (*Accu-Cut* hearts, *Dayco* letters) • Pop dots • ¹/₁₆" hole punch • Needle

Borders give pages pizazz and these ideas are sure to be a hit. Let your ideas fly and use them to decorate gift boxes or bags.

HEART PATTERNS
© Accu-Cut®

Borders

by Katrina Hogan

Hearts Border - MATERIALS: Red cardstock • *F&M Enterprises* film on a roll • Two *Dress It Up* heart buttons • Heart confetti • Red embroidery floss • ¹/₁₆" hole punch • Needle

More border ideas! Use these designs for garlands, table runner trim or border trim in a room. What fun!

by Katrina Hogan

Christmas Tags Border - MATERIALS: Green cardstock • *K & Company* Gold vellum • *Sonburn* Christmas paper • 4 *Making Memories* tags • *Jolee's* Christmas stickers • 4 Gold jump rings • 1/16" hole punch

Leaf Border - MATERIALS: *Close to my Heart* cardstock (Gold, Green, Burgundy) • *Close to my Heart* leaf rubber stamp • Black ink pad • 6 Brass mini brads • Green, Yellow, Red Chalk

Seagulls Border - MATERIALS: *Close to my Heart* cardstock (Brown textured, Blue) • *Magic Scraps* shells • 2 *Dress It Up* seagull buttons

Plastic film adds a 'quacky' quirk to a page when you use it for a shower curtain.

by Laura Gregory

Splish, Splash - MATERIALS: *Bazzill* cardstock (Yellow, Turquoise) • *Design Originals* Splish Splash paper • Silver stripe paper • *F&M Enterprises* Film on a roll • *Stop N Crop* fibers • 8" of ⅛" White ribbon • 5 split rings • *Z Barten* Party ice glitter • *Two Busy Moms* duck sticker • 5 Silver flower eyelets • Eyelet setter • ⅛" hole punch • Die-cuts (*Accu-Cut* tub and people, *Sizzix* letters) • Pop dots • Pink and Blue chalk • Black pen • Glue

PEOPLE PATTERN
© Accu-Cut®

TUB PATTERN
© Accu-Cut®

Bib - MATERIALS: *Lasting Impressions* Yellow check paper • Die-cut heart • Pop dot

by Katrina Hogan

Ribbon Tag - MATERIALS: *Close to my Heart* Yellow cardstock • Purple foil • *Anna Griffin* Red ribbon • *Lasting Impressions* Brass butterfly stencil • Stylus

by Ruth Ann Warwick

Chair - MATERIALS: *Bazzill* cardstock (Green stripe, Ivory) • *Mrs. Grossman's* bear sticker • *Accu-Cut* die-cut chair • Corner punch • Pop dots • Green chalk • Green pen

by Ruth Ann Warwick & Christy Lemond

Cake - MATERIALS: Cardstock (Lavender, Turquoise, Lime Green) • *My Minds Eye* candle die-cut

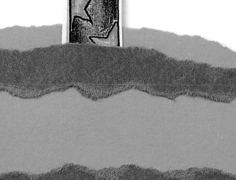

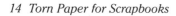

Shapes

Adorable torn shapes are sure to find a home in your favorite scrapbook pages from baby to pets to picnics.

by Ruth Ann Warwick
Cat - MATERIALS: *Lasting Impressions* charcoal print paper • 2 *Westrim* 4mm Gold rhinestones

by Ruth Ann Warwick
Heart - MATERIALS: *Bazzill* Red cardstock • *Sonburn* Red stripe paper

by Ruth Ann Warwick
Hamburger - MATERIALS: Cardstock (Tan, Yellow, Brown, Red, Green) • Brown chalk

Torn Shapes

Fly a flag on a patriotic page, include a telephone for a teenager or plant a tree for a new home… the possibilities are endless!

by Katrina Hogan

Flag - MATERIALS: Cardstock (Blue, Red, Oatmeal) • 18 *Westrim* 4mm Clear rhinestones

by Ruth Ann Warwick

Rattle - MATERIALS: *Bazzill* Light Green cardstock • Pastel plaid paper • 8" of ⅛" Pink satin ribbon • Yellow Chalk

by Ruth Ann Warwick

Telephone - MATERIALS: *Bazzill* cardstock (Black, Silver) • *Worldwin* vellum • 8" of Black elastic cord

by Ruth Ann Warwick
Book - MATERIALS: *Bazzill* cardstock (Navy Blue, Gold, White)

by Ruth Ann Warwick
Carrots - MATERIALS: *Bazzill* cardstock (Green, Dark Green) • *Lasting Impressions* Orange dot paper • Orange and Green chalk

by Ruth Ann Warwick
Basket - MATERIALS: *Keeping Memories Alive* Tan check cardstock • 2 Tan eyelets • Eyelet setter • 1/8" hole punch • Tan chalk

by Ruth Ann Warwick
Tree - MATERIALS: *Bazzill* cardstock (Brown, Red) • *Keeping Memories Alive* paper (Green plaid, Green check) • 1/2" apple punch • Pop dots

Torn Alphabet - MATERIALS: Cardstock, paper or vellum • Die-cut letters or letter template • Craft knife.
TIPS: Cut letters with die cutter or use a template and craft knife. Tear around the edges. Or tear letters freehand.

DIAPER PIN PATTERN
© Accu-Cut®

BABY BIB PATTERN
© Accu-Cut®

Torn Alphabets

What could be easier or more effective than a torn alphabet? This technique will lend itself to many intriguing page creations.

by Laura Gregory

Baby - MATERIALS: *Bazzill* cardstock (Dark Pink, White) • *Worldwin* Metallic Pink paper • *Over the Moon Press* paper (Pink check, Pink star) • *Accu-Cut* die-cuts (Lavender baby bottle, Pink pin, Blue bib) • 4 White ½" buttons • *Stop N Crop* Clear marble and White paper covered wire • Computer generated 'precious' • Pop dots • Brown, Pink chalk

Make great letters!

BABY BOTTLE
PATTERN
© Accu-Cut®

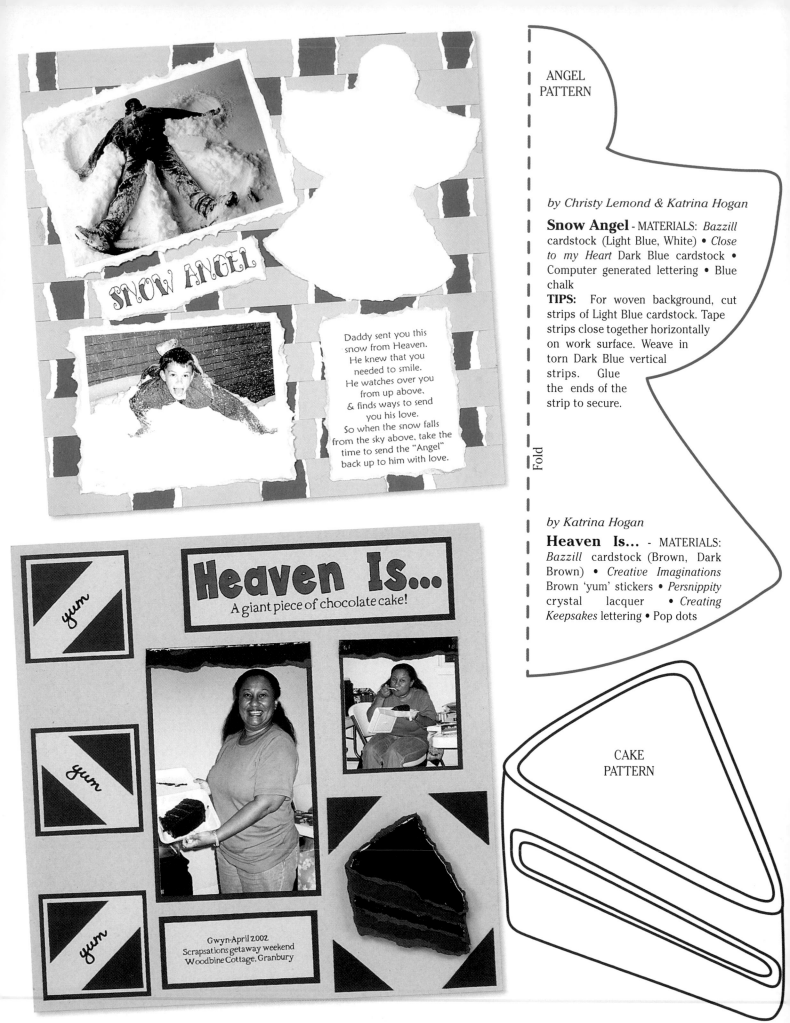

SNOW ANGEL

Daddy sent you this
snow from Heaven.
He knew that you
needed to smile.
He watches over you
from up above,
& finds ways to send
you his love.
So when the snow falls
from the sky above, take the
time to send the "Angel"
back up to him with love.

ANGEL
PATTERN

Fold

by Christy Lemond & Katrina Hogan

Snow Angel - MATERIALS: *Bazzill*
cardstock (Light Blue, White) • *Close
to my Heart* Dark Blue cardstock •
Computer generated lettering • Blue
chalk
TIPS: For woven background, cut
strips of Light Blue cardstock. Tape
strips close together horizontally
on work surface. Weave in
torn Dark Blue vertical
strips. Glue
the ends of the
strip to secure.

by Katrina Hogan

Heaven Is... - MATERIALS:
Bazzill cardstock (Brown, Dark
Brown) • *Creative Imaginations*
Brown 'yum' stickers • *Persnippity*
crystal lacquer • *Creating
Keepsakes* lettering • Pop dots

Heaven Is...
A giant piece of chocolate cake!

yum

yum

yum

Gwyn·April 2002
Scrapsations getaway weekend
Woodbine Cottage, Granbury

CAKE
PATTERN

HAT PATTERN

HAT BRIM PATTERN

HEAD PATTERN

BODY PATTERN

BODY PATTERN

FACE PATTERN

BUTTON PATTERN

ARM PATTERNS

Weave a torn paper background, add crystal icing to a cake slice or construct a perky snowman… every embellishment you use makes the page extraordinary!

by Christy Lemond

Snow Day - MATERIALS: *Bazzill* cardstock (White, Black, Blue, Brown, Blue dot, Orange dot) • *Creative Imaginations* snowflake print paper • *Sizzix* die cutter • 1½" letter dies • ¼" hole punch • Pink and Blue chalk

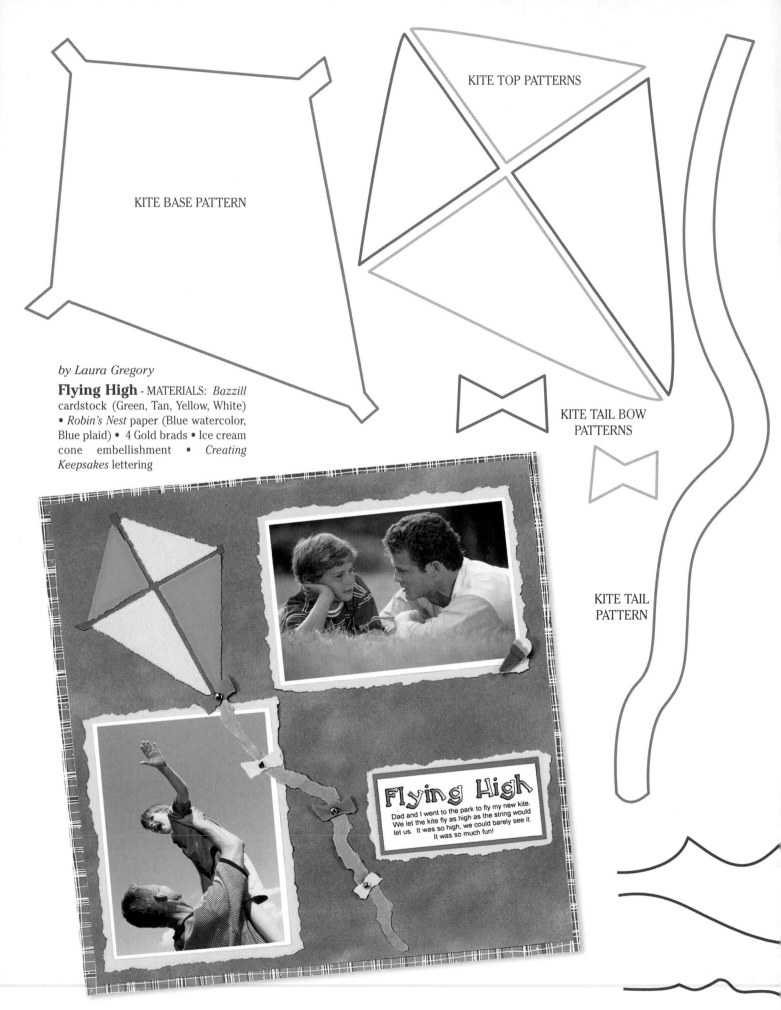

KITE TOP PATTERNS

KITE BASE PATTERN

KITE TAIL BOW PATTERNS

KITE TAIL PATTERN

by Laura Gregory

Flying High - MATERIALS: *Bazzill* cardstock (Green, Tan, Yellow, White) • *Robin's Nest* paper (Blue watercolor, Blue plaid) • 4 Gold brads • Ice cream cone embellishment • *Creating Keepsakes* lettering

Flying High

Dad and I went to the park to fly my new kite. We let the kite fly as high as the string would let us. It was so high, we could barely see it. It was so much fun!

Fun Days

Summer fun means flying high with a kite or spending the day at the beach. Keep the memories alive with brightly colored pages.

by Christy Lemond

Summer 2002 - MATERIALS: *Bazzill* cardstock (Gold, White. Light Blue) • *Paper Adventures* Dark Blue paper • *Wubie Prints* sky vellum • *Deluxe Cuts* Black and White Orca die-cuts • Gold chalk

Summer 2002

Jason floated while we went down the water slides...

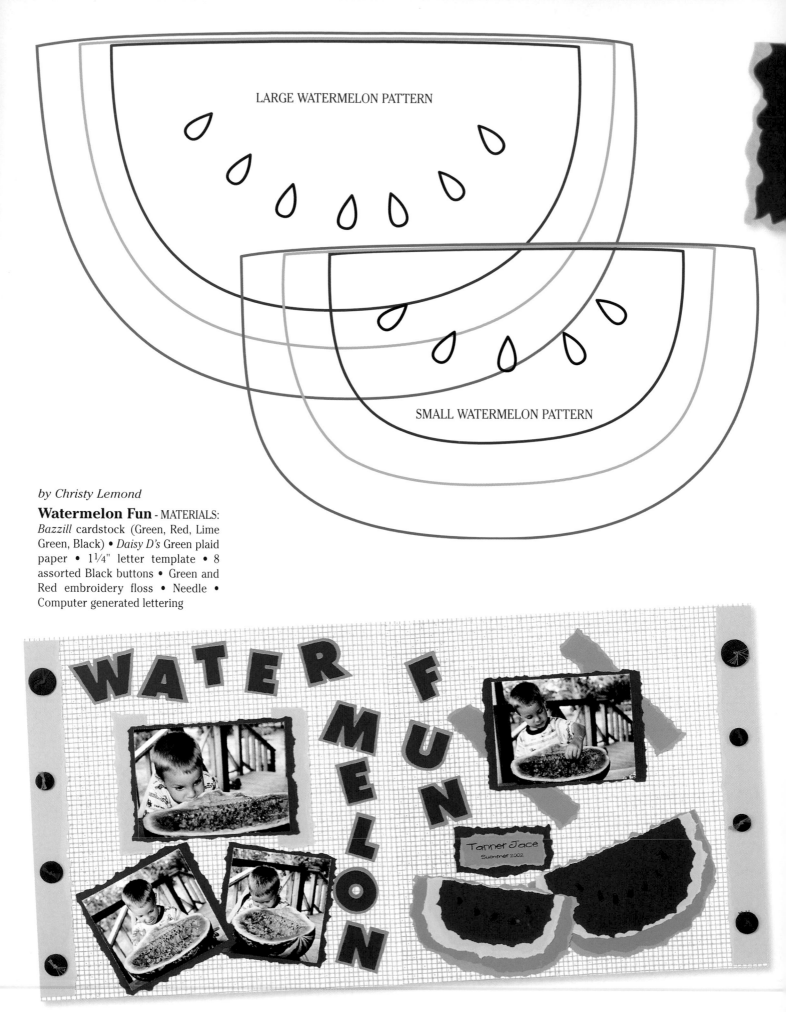

LARGE WATERMELON PATTERN

SMALL WATERMELON PATTERN

by Christy Lemond

Watermelon Fun - MATERIALS: *Bazzill* cardstock (Green, Red, Lime Green, Black) • *Daisy D's* Green plaid paper • 1¼" letter template • 8 assorted Black buttons • Green and Red embroidery floss • Needle • Computer generated lettering

Sweet Days

Slurpy watermelon kids and angelic sleeping babies make cherished childhood memories.

BALLOON PATTERN

HEAD PATTERN

BEAK PATTERN

BODY PATTERN

FEET PATTERNS

by Ruth Ann Warwick

Baby Jace - MATERIALS: *Bazzill* cardstock (Light Yellow, Yellow, Light Green, Blue, Gold) • *Keeping Memories Alive* Yellow dot paper • *Dayco* 1½" letter die-cuts • White fiber • 2 Blue 3mm rhinestones • Chalk (Blue, Yellow, Green)

Torn paper shapes add wonderful texture and visual excitement to your scrapbook pages! Anything goes!

by Christy Lemond

Wild Thing - MATERIALS: *Bazzill* cardstock (Black, White) • *Worldwin* Red vellum • *Stamping Station* Silver die-cut • *Creative Imaginations* 13/16" Black letter stickers

Wild thing...
You make
my heart
sing!

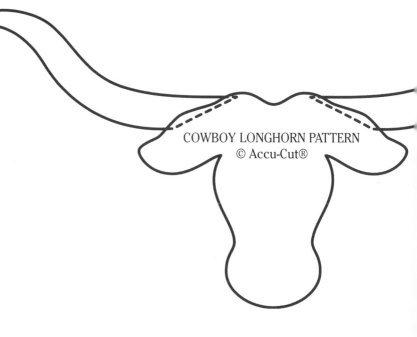

COWBOY LONGHORN PATTERN
© Accu-Cut®

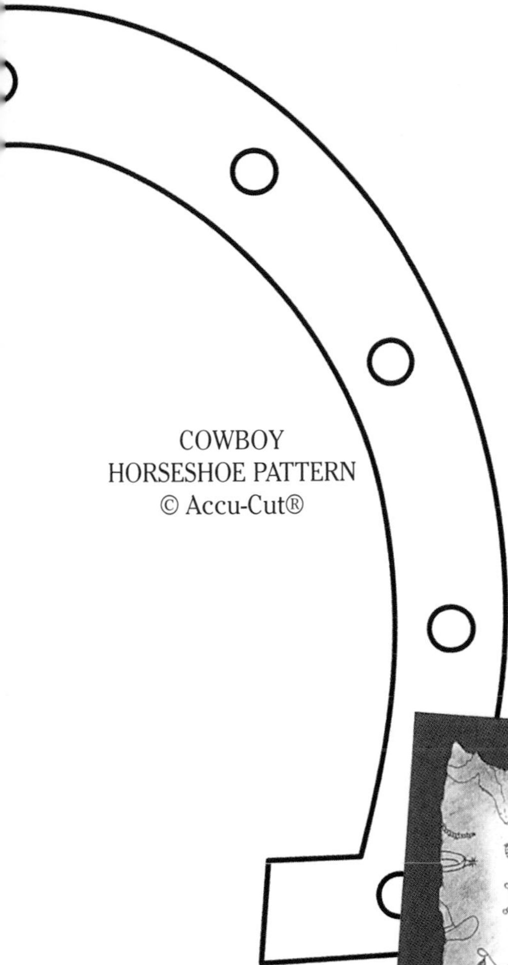

Playing Grown Up

COWBOY
HORSESHOE PATTERN
© Accu-Cut®

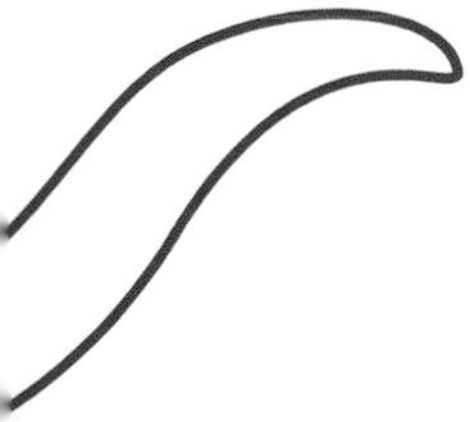

Our children give us our most unforgettable memories. Keep them fresh in your walk down memory lane album!

by Ruth Ann Warwick

Cowboy - MATERIALS: *Bazzill* cardstock (Brown, Light Brown, Tan, Ivory) • *Pixie Press* print paper • 9 *Scrapbook Studios* Gold rivets • *Accu-Cut* horseshoe and longhorn die-cuts • Foam mounting tape • Brown and Black chalk • Black pen

There is nothing more fun than the 4th of July or a day at the park. These pages are as brilliant and bright as summer days!

by Christy Lemond

July 4th - MATERIALS: *Bazzill* cardstock (Black, White textured) • Handmade paper (Red, White, Blue) • *Sizzix* die cutter • Letter and number dies • Black and Yellow Twistel • 4 *Eyelet Factory* White star eyelets • Eyelet setter • 1/8" hole punch • Pop dots • Black pen

FIRECRACKER BASE PATTERN

How to Braid Border Strips

1. Wet paper, crumple into a ball and smooth out.

2. Place paper on flat surface to dry. Tear into strips.

3. Staple ends of strips together and braid. Staple finished braid to secure. Do not tear paper.

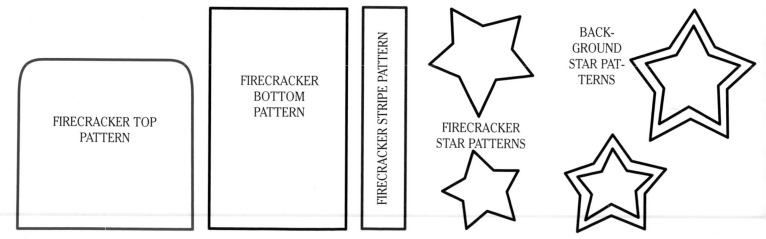

FIRECRACKER TOP PATTERN

FIRECRACKER BOTTOM PATTERN

FIRECRACKER STRIPE PATTERN

FIRECRACKER STAR PATTERNS

BACK-GROUND STAR PATTERNS

Pages

PLANE
PATTERN

by Ruth Ann Warwick

Just Plane Cute - MATERIALS: *Bazzill* cardstock (Red, Yellow, Blue, Light Blue, White, Black) • *Creating Keepsakes* lettering • White gel pen

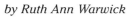

Color explodes on these delightful Torn Paper Art pages!

Jace Warwick 3 years old

Fort Worth Texas

Just Plane Cute

Whether your child is a cowboy, fisherman or a little lady, make pages filled with their lively personalities.

by Christy Lemond

Ropin' Time - MATERIALS: *Bazzill* cardstock (Black, Tan) • *Carolee's Creations* bandana print paper • Eyelets (2 *Eyelet Factory* Black stars, 4 *Making Memories* Black square eyelets) • 3 *ScrapKings* Black nail heads • Jute • Computer generated lettering • Pop dots • Brown chalk

by Laura Gregory

Emily - MATERIALS: *Bazzill* cardstock (Light Gold, Brown) • Paper (*Lasting Impressions* Gold dot, *Paper Patch* bee print) • White Magic Mesh • *Creative Imaginations* ¾" Black letter stickers • Black pen

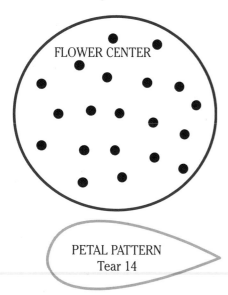

FLOWER CENTER

PETAL PATTERN
Tear 14

Plus +

My Fisherman

FISH
PATTERN

BODY SCALE
PATTERNS

SLIT

TEAR
TAIL

TOP FIN
PATTERN

BOTTOM
FIN
PATTERN

FISH HOOK
PATTERN
© Accu-Cut®

BOBBER
PATTERN

BOBBER
PATTERN

FISHING ROD PATTERN © Accu-Cut®

by Ruth Ann Warwick

My Fisherman
MATERIALS: *SEI* paper (White, Red, Light Green, Pale Blue, Gray marble) • *Worldwin* Green vellum • *Accu-Cut* fishing rod and fish hook die-cuts • 10mm Clear rhinestone • 26 gauge Teal wire • *Creating Keepsakes* lettering • Green chalk

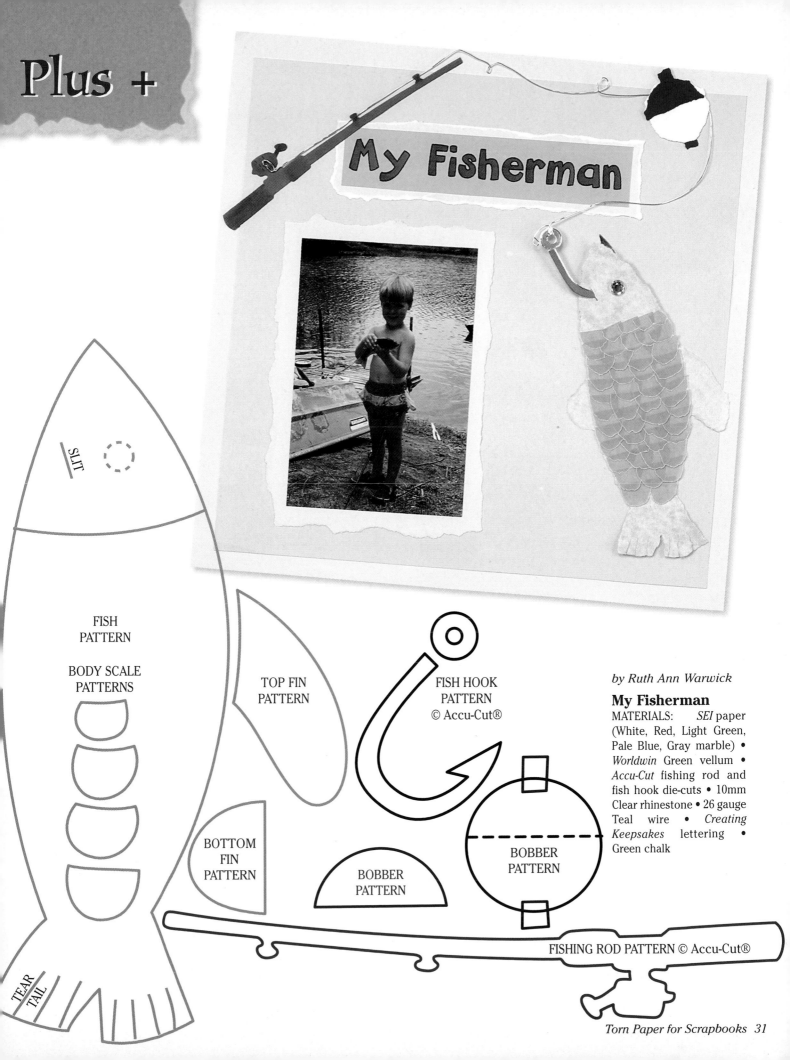

Christmas Time

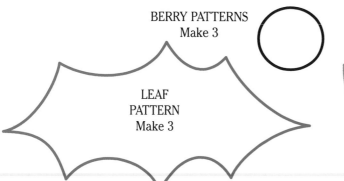

by Christy Lemond

Tanner & Santa - MATERIALS: *Bazzill* cardstock (White, Red, Green) • Paper (*Creative Imaginations* Red dot, *Keeping Memories Alive* Green check) • 4 *Making Memories* White buttons • Red Twistel • Green and Gray chalk • Green pen

BERRY PATTERNS
Make 3

LEAF
PATTERN
Make 3

Fold

Fold

HOLLY PATTERNS

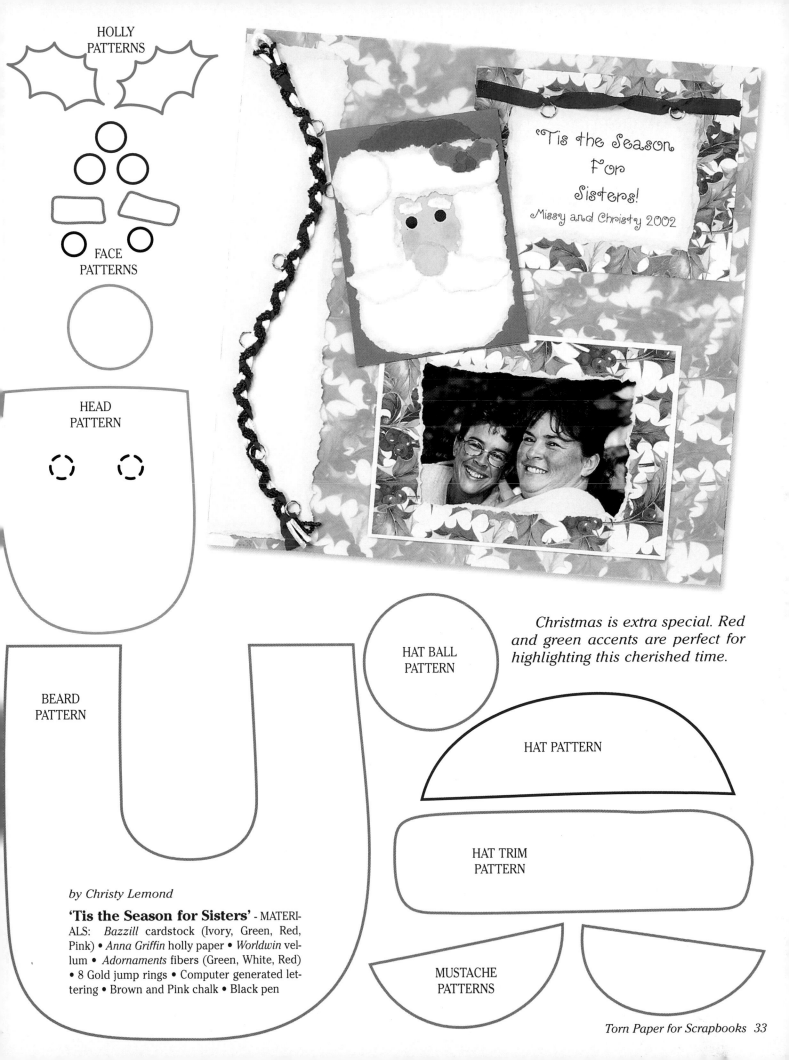

FACE PATTERNS

HEAD PATTERN

BEARD PATTERN

HAT BALL PATTERN

HAT PATTERN

HAT TRIM PATTERN

MUSTACHE PATTERNS

'Tis the Season
For
Sisters!
Missy and Christy 2002

Christmas is extra special. Red and green accents are perfect for highlighting this cherished time.

by Christy Lemond

'Tis the Season for Sisters' - MATERIALS: *Bazzill* cardstock (Ivory, Green, Red, Pink) • *Anna Griffin* holly paper • *Worldwin* vellum • *Adornaments* fibers (Green, White, Red) • 8 Gold jump rings • Computer generated lettering • Brown and Pink chalk • Black pen

Adventure Time

by Ruth Ann Warwick & Laura Gregory

Indiana - MATERIALS: *Bazzill* cardstock (Green, Dark Green, Dark Sage Green, Brown) • *Worldwin* Ivory vellum • Print paper (*Creative Imaginations, Hot Off the Press, Paper Adventures*) • *Far & Away* page title • *Adornaments* Green fibers • *Scrappin' Fools* Gold grommets • Jute • Foam mounting tape • Green Crystal lacquer

Party like a pirate or go adventuring together… remember the warm, fuzzy feeling forever!

TREE PATTERNS

Torn Paper adds creative ideas to make scrapbooks a fun experience!